In Aunt Giraffe's Green Garden

JACK PRELUTSKY

In Aunt Giraffe's Green Garden

PICTURES BY
PETRA MATHERS

Library of Congress Cataloging-in-Publication Data
Prelutsky, Jack.
In Aunt Giraffe's green garden / rhymes by Jack Prelutsky ;
pictures by Petra Mathers.
p.   cm.
"Greenwillow Books."
ISBN-13: 978-0-06-623868-5 (trade bdg.) ISBN-10: 0-06-623868-4 (trade bdg.)
ISBN-13: 978-0-06-623869-2 (lib. bdg.) ISBN-10: 0-06-623869-2 (lib. bdg.)
1. Animals—Juvenile poetry. 2. Children's poetry, American. I. Mathers, Petra, ill. II. Title.
PS3566.R36I5 2007 811'.54—dc22 2005035928

First Edition 10 9 8 7 6 5 4 3 2 1

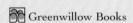 Greenwillow Books

To Brigitte and Celeste
—J. P.

For Jacob,
cute as a bug's ear
—P. M.

CONTENTS

IN AUNT GIRAFFE'S GREEN GARDEN

In Aunt Giraffe's green garden,
the flowers are so tall
that when she stops to sniff them,
she scarcely stoops at all.

The bugs, who love to climb them,
are careful not to fall
back down into the garden,
where everything is tall.

9

TEN MICE WENT TO DENVER

Ten mice went to Denver
and stayed there for weeks
to gaze at the Rockies'
magnificent peaks.

With snow on their summits,
they made a grand sight—
the mice were so happy
they squeaked day and night.

A BIG BLUE GOOSE
AND A LITTLE GREEN DUCK

A big blue goose and a little green duck
drove around in a rusty truck,
a rusty truck with a rusty chassis,
from Detroit to Tallahassee.

Then they headed for the coast,
eating bits of buttered toast.
In Miami they sipped juice,
the little green duck and the big blue goose.

13

IN THE SPRING IN KANSAS CITY

In the spring in Kansas City,
Casey raced along the ground.
Then she jumped into a fountain,
where she gaily splashed around.

All day long in Kansas City,
Casey frolicked to and fro—
when she headed home that evening,
she was wet from head to toe.

15

SLEEPY SAM

Sleepy Sam, the sleepyhead,
slept all morning in his bed,
slept as well all afternoon—
when he woke, he saw the moon.

He arose at nine that night,
just to have himself a bite.
When he'd had his bread and jam,
back to bed went sleepy Sam.

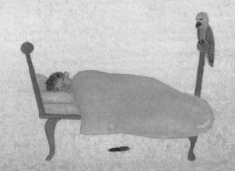

I WENT TO CHEYENNE

I went to Cheyenne
for a day and a half,
to ride a wild pony,
to rope a wild calf.
The pony bucked hard—
I did not stand a chance,
and soon landed down
on the seat of my pants.

That pony laughed loud
as I sat in the dirt,
not one bit impressed
by my fine cowboy shirt.
The calf ran away
when the roundup began—
that's what went on
when I went to Cheyenne.

THE POODLES ATE OODLES OF NOODLES

The poodles ate oodles of noodles,
the setters ate lettuce on rye.
A small Pekingese
ate nothing but peas,
and a greyhound ran off with the pie.

THE SNOW FELL IN BILLINGS

The snow fell in Billings
one blustery day—
though winter was over,
it fell anyway.

The children rushed out
of their houses to play
in mountains of snow
in the middle of May.

23

ABOVE THE WIDE POTOMAC

Above the wide Potomac,
majestic eagles fly,
they swoop and soar all morning
in the clear Virginia sky.

Then to awaiting treetops
they make a swift descent,
near beautiful Mount Vernon,
home of our first president.

THIS IS WHAT HAPPENED

This is what happened
one bright summer day—
a duck and a donkey
decided to play.
They raced and they wrestled,
and though it was fun,
the donkey soon noticed
the duck always won.

They tried playing checkers,
jacks, hopscotch, and tag.
The duck kept on winning . . .
it started to brag.
The donkey, defeated,
replied with a bray,
and that is what happened
one bright summer day.

THERE WAS A LITTLE CRICKET

There was a little cricket
in the deep green wood
that wasn't very naughty,
and wasn't very good.
It wasn't very timid,
and it wasn't very bold,
it wasn't very young,
and it wasn't very old.

It lived in a thicket
in the middle of the trees,
listening to music
with its little cricket knees,
singing just as loud
as a little cricket could—
that happy little cricket
in the deep green wood.

29

IN AMARILLO, TEXAS

In Amarillo, Texas,
upon a yellow chair,
complete with yellow pillow,
sat little Willa Ware.

She ate a yellow apple,
she ate a yellow pear,
while wearing yellow flowers
atop her yellow hair.

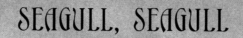

SEAGULL, SEAGULL

Seagull, seagull,
hover, glide,
high above
the ocean tide.

Seagull, seagull,
come ashore,
spend the day
in Baltimore.

IN TOLEDO

In Toledo, four fat geese
waddled up and down.
One was dressed in woolen fleece,
one goose wore a gown.

One goose wore a silken shirt
striped with white and red,
one goose had a stocking cap
fastened to her head.

All day long they marched about,
acting puffed and proud.
All day long they sang a song,
honking very loud.

Everybody held their ears,
wishing they would cease.
But they sang till dinnertime,
four Toledo geese.

THERE'S A LADY IN GALOSHES

There's a lady in galoshes,
and her name is Jolly Jane.
How she loves to look for lobsters
on the rocky coast of Maine.

She can find them by the dozen
in the sun and wind and rain.
She's the queen of lobster ladies,
and her name is Jolly Jane.

DANCING DOT AND DANCING DAN

Dancing Dot and Dancing Dan
danced all autumn in Spokane.
They were light upon their feet
as they danced upon the street.

In Spokane, as leaves fell down,
they kept dancing through the town.
But when it began to snow,
they danced off to Idaho.

39

HIGH
ATOP A
LOFTY MOUNTAIN

High atop a lofty mountain
all the morning long,
a contented little bluebird
chirped a cheery song.

No one else was there to hear it
as it sang away,
happy just to be a bluebird
on a lovely day.

RUN, LITTLE RED FOX

Run, little red fox,
red fox run.
Run through the meadow
under the sun.
Race through the flowers
quick as you please,
streak through the forest,
weave through the trees.

Run, little red fox,
run to your den.
Get to your home
by half past ten.
Be in your bed
when the day is done —
run, little red fox,
red fox run.

ON A MANGROVE TREE

On a mangrove tree, a grackle
glances at a frog
studying an alligator
looking like a log.

Flocks of egrets fish for dinner
as the daylight fades,
and a turtle swims in circles
in the Everglades.

44

SALLY, SALLY

Sally, Sally, you're so silly.
What are you about—
sitting on a water lily,
calling to a trout?

Silly Sally, how you dally.
Why are you so fond
of your lily, silly Sally,
on the lily pond?

47

THERE WAS A MAN IN MEXICO

There was a man in Mexico
who dearly loved to draw.
He drew enchanting pictures
of the many things he saw.
His pen was filled with magic,
so his drawings came alive—
one day he drew a bumblebee
that buzzed off to a hive.

He drew a hippopotamus,
a rabbit, and a mouse
that climbed down from his drawing pad
and marched about his house.
He drew a frog that hopped around
and played a piccolo—
he did this in the town
of Guanajuato, Mexico.

IN BEMIDJI, MINNESOTA

In Bemidji, Minnesota,
Ida sat upon the ice,
fishing on a frosty morning,
and she shivered once or twice.

Just to catch a fish for supper
was her single, silent wish. . . .
In Bemidji, Minnesota,
Ida caught a frozen fish.

ON A POND, A SILENT SWAN

On a pond, a silent swan
glided softly on and on.
All day long, without a sound,
that one swan swam all around.

When the sun set in the sky,
that one swan still glided by.
When the night was dark and deep,
that one swan was fast asleep.

IN NORTH CAROLINA

In North Carolina,
not far from the sea,
a pig and a pigeon
sat under a tree.
The pigeon told tales
of exploring the sky.
The pig said, "Dear pigeon,
please teach me to fly."

The pigeon replied
to this foolish request,
"A pig cannot learn
what I learned in the nest."
The pig nodded sadly,
and had to agree,
in North Carolina,
not far from the sea.

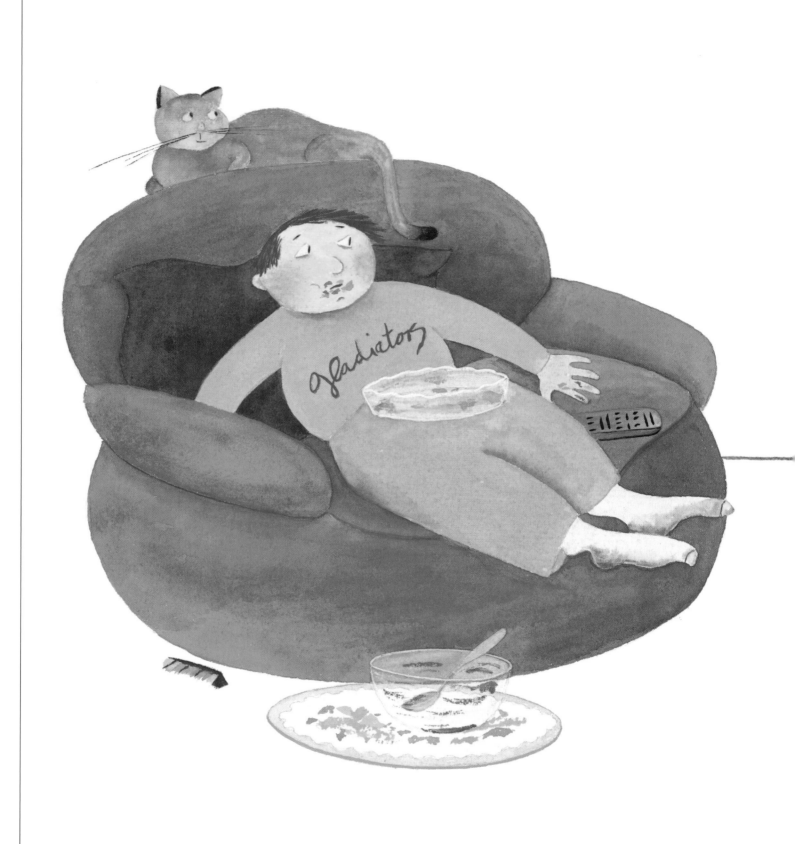

PETER ATE A POUND OF PUDDING

Peter ate a pound of pudding
and a pumpkin pie,
Peter ate a layer cake
eleven inches high.

Peter ate a cookie
that was bigger than his cat.
He never ate his spinach—
Peter had no room for that.

LITTLE BAT, LITTLE BAT

Little bat, little bat
in your cave,
sleeping all day long.
You don't see the birds outside,
you can't hear their song.

Little bat, little bat
upside down,
while the sun is high . . .
when the stars are out tonight,
you'll be in the sky.

60

IN LA JOLLA, CALIFORNIA

In La Jolla, California,
Susu sat upon the sand,
watching with a sense of wonder
how the water washed the land.

Susu saw, above the ocean,
pelicans in graceful flight.
In La Jolla, California,
Susu laughed with great delight.

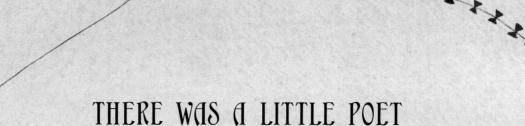

THERE WAS A LITTLE POET

There was a little poet
with a little silver pen,
who liked to write a little,
every little now and then.
He took a little journey
to a little mountain stream,
and there he took a little nap
and dreamed a little dream.

He dreamed of little dragons,
and he dreamed of little kings,
he dreamed of little elephants
with little golden wings.
He woke a little later
and he thought a little while,
then wrote a book of little rhymes
and smiled a little smile.

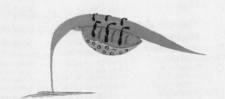

Jack Prelutsky is the nation's first Children's Poet Laureate. His poems are recited, laughed over, and memorized by children across the country. His inventive wordplay and unpredictable rhymes have appeared in such favorites as *The New Kid on the Block*, *Something Big Has Been Here*, *A Pizza the Size of the Sun*, and *It's Raining Pigs & Noodles*. For younger readers his work includes three companions to this book: *Ride a Purple Pelican* and *Beneath a Blue Umbrella*, both illustrated by Garth Williams; and *The Frogs Wore Red Suspenders*, illustrated by Petra Mathers.

Petra Mathers has written and illustrated many books for children, most recently her very popular "Lottie's World" series.

She lives with her husband, Michael, beside the mighty Columbia River in Oregon.